Six-Word Lessons to

THINK LIKE A MODERN-DAY CIO

100 Lessons CIOs and Tech Leaders Must Embrace to Drive Business Velocity

Jim DuBois

Former Microsoft CIO

Published by Pacelli Publishing
Bellevue, Washington

Six-Word Lessons to Think Like a Modern-Day CIO

Published by Pacelli Publishing
9905 Lake Washington Blvd. NE, #D-103
Bellevue, Washington 98004
PacelliPublishing.com

Cover and interior designed by Pacelli Publishing
Cover image by Pixabay.com

ISBN-10: 1-933750-65-0
ISBN-13: 978-1-933750-65-1

Contents

Introduction

When I was asked to be CIO at Microsoft in 2013, I knew I had a daunting task ahead of me, but I had no idea of the radical change that was about to hit. A CEO transition and acquisitions of Nokia and LinkedIn were just the tip of the iceberg. Historic IT mindsets were slowing us down at a time when we needed speed. Legacy systems and processes seemed to have a mind of their own. I asked my team for help in accelerating everything we were trying to do -- some people embraced the opportunity, and others resisted. We broke some things, made mistakes, but we learned. After eventually making considerable progress over a few years, I found myself looking back at everything we figured out. I wished I could take the lessons and start over. I could go so much faster with far fewer missteps, and be further along on the journey with less churn. Given that starting over wasn't realistic, I decided I could at least write down some of the biggest lessons for others starting with this book.

If the world around us was static, you would not need many of these lessons. Unfortunately, or maybe fortunately, our world today is evolving faster than ever. You can no longer work the way we were taught in school or by our predecessors. You can help others around you realize this, or wait for someone else to step up. You can play a leadership role regardless of where you are in your organization. Just working smarter isn't enough. We need to break some rules and change how we approach our mission in order to push the pace and help our businesses transform while still having a good balance to our lives.

While I may have learned faster as an avid reader of the latest trends, most of the lessons in this book are drawn from mistakes I made and had to figure out throughout my career. Every step of the way, and long before I became CIO, I had leaders who challenged me to think beyond what I believed was possible, to move faster than I thought was safe. If you are not feeling pushed, find a mentor who will push you out of your comfort zone.

I didn't always have the answer, but drove forward without giving up until we succeeded. This helped me improve. I did get a lot wrong, sometimes dramatically, but we would not have made as much progress if we hadn't tried and learned. In striving to bring more people along with me, I know there were times I didn't make decisions fast enough. But we had to keep going. With the aspirations Microsoft had to scale, with the target we became for security attacks, and with the agility our business needed to innovate, we had to go beyond industry best practices and find new ways of working. We were compelled to adopt from companies born in the cloud, and apply lessons to a very large enterprise with significant legacy systems and processes.

I believe that what we learned applies to any team trying to transform using technology today, whether that team is large or small, inside formal IT boundaries or within a department of an organization outside IT. I hope these lessons give you ideas, allowing you to accomplish everything you need faster in a world that demands speed to thrive. The goal isn't about making IT go faster. It is about changing IT to help drive the pace for company-wide digital transformations.

Chapter One

Build a Culture
That Supports Change

I got to experience the culture of three very different CEOs at Microsoft.

In 1993, my very first project was to modernize our IT systems off our legacy DEC VAX and IBM AS400 environment. We picked SAP as the software package to implement on a Windows Server environment. In those days, a project of this magnitude had to be approved by Bill Gates directly.

The approval meeting only lasted a few minutes because Bill looked ahead in the deck we passed out, and before we'd really begun the meeting he said, "Wait a minute.

Millions of dollars to implement a software package? Are you serious?"

His exact words were more colorful, but he killed the project. Fortunately, we were empowered to rethink our strategy, allowing us to implement SAP in smaller projects that paid for themselves as we went, and likely allowing us to go faster than a big bang effort. Lessons like this started to change how I approached IT, but change was slow.

With Steve Ballmer as CEO the company continued to grow, but the culture changed and became more siloed since all major decisions did not have to go through Bill. I remember a customer experience meeting we had with Steve, where he was visibly frustrated he couldn't immediately solve cross product customer issues we raised. He wanted to, but would have needed to override the priorities he'd set for separate product teams.

I watched Satya Nadella learn from the different cultures under Bill and Steve. When he took the reins as CEO, he took the best of both and added his own magic to inspire everyone to want to work together. I realized from watching how Satya drove his company-wide transformation, that I was also fighting culture. Historic thinking about IT, both inside my organization and how we interacted with the rest of the company, was bogging down the change I was pushing. In addition to the mindset change, we needed to strengthen some people skills. We had tried learning how to collaborate better as a company, and I was struggling with this in my own organization. As we tried to transform the old Microsoft traits into new, there were a lot of people who liked the sounds of what Satya was evangelizing:

changing from knowers to learners, from trying to prove that you are the smartest, to trying to understand what our customers need and to be curious about diverse perspectives. But it wasn't easy and there were missteps as people learned. Some people would call you out for not collaborating if you didn't agree with them. Or on the other extreme people became so respectful that they avoided difficult discussions. I learned that collaboration requires both working respectfully and achieving a positive outcome together. To make progress quickly we could never avoid the discussions that needed to be resolved, but how they were addressed was important. These were skills we needed to improve, but the culture had to support the change, and no longer value the old ways. Without the purposeful drive to change culture, we could have never made as much progress.

1

Culture does eat strategy for breakfast.

I learned from Satya Nadella that culture really is more important than strategy, or vision, or any of the other things taught in business school. I intentionally start with this lesson because it is the foundation for everything else. If the culture in your organization loves the status quo and does not like making material changes quickly, the culture will fight against the changes you are trying to make and will slow everything down. Spend time on purposefully defining and building the culture and values you need.

The future belongs to the fast.

I've heard this repeated often in the last few years, and determined that I did not want to be left behind. I learned to bring my team along, leveraging those who were ready, and helping the rest understand that the new faster pace is not going to slow down. Our faster pace is the new normal. Companies cannot thrive by operating like they did in the past. Team culture needs to embrace the transformation and accept the changes in order to thrive in the modern world.

Adopt startup lessons.
Experiment. Fail fast.

Speed requires working differently. Startup cultures don't figure everything out before they begin. We can learn from them. Create a hypothesis for how you can accelerate progress. Define how to measure it. Conduct experiments, and stop quickly if the experiment isn't helpful. Learn and adjust to make progress. Leverage the results and ideas from everyone on the team to make more progress. This is a significant culture change from yesterday's IT.

Be fast, but don't hurry (plan).

If you never fail, you probably aren't going fast enough, but you still need to plan. In fact planning might be even more important when you go fast, but plans must now be flexible to change as you learn. Fast comes with more risk, which you accept by better managing the risk. Create excellent contingency plans. Create urgency. Go fast, but make sure you can detect failure early and recover quickly. How you respond to failure will change your team's behavior. Encourage risk-taking by celebrating the learning from any failure.

Insist your culture supports data-driven decisions.

Create a culture where everyone expects to need data to support any decision. Take opinion, and the corresponding needless debate, out of decision-making to eliminate wasting time. If there isn't clear data, do an experiment rather than attempt a lasting decision, but don't wait. Appreciate collecting data even where you aren't positive of its value yet. Teams will learn new value as they apply data to decisions and experiments. As Peter Drucker said, "You can't improve what you can't measure."

Value growth mindsets over fixed mindsets.

Everyone wanting to modernize should read Carol Dweck's book *Mindset*. She explains the difference between growth mindsets (always seeking to learn and improve) over fixed mindsets (knowing the ways things have always worked). Everyone has some of both. Cultivate more of a growth mindset as critical to your new culture and future. Tear down the barriers of the past. Be curious. Accelerate your learning.

Ensure your culture supports healthy escalations.

People should not feel like they failed if they need to escalate. Healthy environments move fast by rapidly determining when an issue won't be resolved right away. All parties agree to escalate together to get leader input. All points of view are included in the escalation. Healthy is undermined if one side escalates alone. Success is not getting your way – success is moving forward.

Promote communication. Build psychologically safe environments.

Healthy escalations help cultivate safe environments where people are encouraged to speak up. To go fast, you must break down historical hierarchies and communication blockers. If employees feel safe, you will get the best ideas, questions for clarity, and criticisms that help you improve. Criticism is a gift. Don't be defensive. Use it to improve.

Help everyone be their best self.

Culture change takes time, but happens faster when everyone really wants it. Make sure you advocate for a culture that people desire. A healthy culture listens for all opinions and points of view, feels inclusive and respectful, and values learning over knowing. It craves self-actualization, individuality, and inclusivity, allowing everyone to leverage their strengths to make a meaningful impact in the world.

10

Real culture change begins with you.

Leaders go first. When actions of leaders do not support the culture you want, bottom-up change won't happen. Leaders must model the desired culture, and help other leaders do the same. Explain the culture to the whole organization, and all stakeholders. Engage the willing to accelerate the change. When leaders model the desired state, those waiting to see progress will join faster.

Chapter Two

Build a Clear and Evolving Vision

For my first three years as CIO, I reported to Kevin Turner. What I most valued from Kevin, even when I didn't like it, was his ability to drive clarity around what success looked like. At times, I didn't feel his vision for success was even possible, and in those times Kevin would ask me if I'd rather aim low and be safe. I knew the answer was no. I don't think we'd have made the same progress without people like Kevin pushing us to be better.

Kevin loved defining a clear vision of success. I know he valued learning because as we transformed, his vision evolved. Kevin had a support staff, trying to optimize his more than 50,000-person organization in over 100 countries. They helped make sure the rest of us didn't stray too far outside the lines, and did it so effectively that many people didn't realize that Kevin completely empowered us to achieve the vision. Kevin told us that Satya was helping him learn to drive accountability with more empathy, but it didn't diminish Kevin's passion around driving for success. He was clear on the difference between activity and outcomes. Outcomes are steps toward the vision. Unless you are driving real learning, activities without results are only excuses. Kevin would say, "If you are justifying, you are losing."

If we encountered a disaster somewhere in the world, Kevin would tell us to "never waste a crisis." Leverage it to make progress. In the face of ambiguity, he would say to "be bold, and be right." I later understood he meant be right as much as possible, because when something didn't work, Kevin would remind me that at our pace, it was impossible to always be right. He would tell me it was more important to keep making measurable progress toward the vision. When Kevin eventually decided to leave Microsoft, while it may have actually helped Satya's transformation because having half the company report to one person was starting to slow us down, we definitely did miss Kevin's ability to drive clarity around real success.

Fast in the wrong direction fails.

Going fast is only useful when there is a clear, compelling vision of where we are going. Not a vision statement, but a rich description that gives meaning to the future, answers the "why" questions, shows us how the business will operate differently, how new value is realized, and how teams will operate better together to deliver these outcomes. This clarity on the direction to run, allows for more team autonomy and empowerment.

Make sure the vision can evolve.

In our dynamic world, this vision cannot be static. It should evolve as you learn. Don't change it dramatically all the time or you will frustrate people; but when you learn something material, or someone has a great idea to improve the vision, do update it and communicate it again. Ensure there is a process for regularly updating all stakeholders to better manage expectations.

13

Remind everyone of the vision regularly.

Once the vision is clear, even when it doesn't change, don't assume that everyone gets it. It needs continual reinforcement for it to sink in. Something stable in a sea of constant change can bring comfort and build confidence. As you build on your vision, and when you update everyone on progress, always start by repeating where you are going.

Define what is inhibiting progress today.

One of the best ways to help everyone understand the vision is to encourage a discussion around where you are not like the vision yet. Explain not only gaps between today and the vision, but a list of what is keeping you from getting there faster. Be curious. Get everyone involved, contributing to, and owning the list to ensure understanding.

15

Define how to measure vision progress.

Another critical way to help people understand the vision is to clearly define the business metric(s) that will be used to measure success--not a list of metrics, but the one or two that really define the progress. These should not be IT metrics related to IT delivery, but the business metrics that will measure the outcomes and the company success.

16

Go after the important problems first.

What changes will make the biggest difference in getting you to the vision? Prioritize the big rocks first. Prioritize new capabilities and simplifications. You understand all this, but make sure you factor in some quick wins, and identify experiments to accelerate. Don't underestimate the value of progress to build momentum and attract more believers to the vision.

17

Clarify the roadmap to the vision.

With a clear vision and view of the priorities, define a roadmap to help people understand milestones along the way. This isn't a locked plan, and no one should expect to follow it exactly. It includes expected milestones for both adding new capabilities, and when legacy will be retired. Update the roadmap as you learn. Create the detail around features and changes needed next to create a healthy, groomed backlog. Communicate the roadmap along with the vision.

18

Identify, clarify and resolve all dependencies.

Beyond clarity for teams, a primary purpose in building roadmaps is dependency management. Understand every dependency, internal or external, especially where they become a critical path for one of the teams. When vision and high-level roadmaps are clear, most of the time spent managing progress becomes resolving dependencies. Make sure details around next dependencies are clear when grooming the backlog.

19

Make issues visible to all teams.

When there is an issue, the natural tendency is to try to resolve it before anyone finds out. Unfortunately, this doesn't allow everyone else to react faster, to help each other, or adjust plans. Broad visibility to issues follows the principle that bad news should travel fast. Make sharing the stuff that hurts a healthy part of your culture. The culture should feel negatively about withholding information.

20

Empower everyone to improve the plan.

Everyone can innovate to improve the solution once you have a shared sense of purpose, and clarity on vision, roadmap, and issues. All can find ways to accelerate the plan, including solving issues faster. It's amazing to see ideas from users that help them achieve results faster, and innovations from developers who now understand why, rather than just coding to requirements.

Chapter Three

Empower Teams to Deliver the Vision

I n early 1998, John Connors was CIO of Microsoft. When we told him we were struggling to get the Windows team to recognize gaps for us in the enterprise version of Windows NT, he arranged a session with Bill Gates so we could give him IT practitioner feedback. We explained to Bill where we needed better manageability, where we had to improve security, and why it was impractical to require a person to sign in at the console rather than remotely.

With every point we raised, Bill told us we must be incompetent if we needed the product to be simpler and more foolproof. I was feeling like this meeting was a waste of everyone's time. That is until the end when Bill turned to the head of Windows and said, "I don't know why these guys think this is so hard, but we need to make this work for our customers as I bet a lot of them will say the same thing. You need to get your team to fix all the items on their list!"

We left the room on a high. Maybe we were incompetent, but Bill got our points, and the products were going to be better for our customers.

Over the years that followed, Steve Ballmer and then Satya Nadella made a practice of coming to IT for feedback, kicked off by this one meeting. And knowing that the CEO cared about our opinion, appropriate product teams engaged with us regularly to better understand enterprise needs.

Like John did in this example, do what is needed to help teams make a difference. Don't be afraid to look silly. Find ways to get around blockers. Do what is right to achieve the vision.

21

Remove all governance barriers and complexities.

Once everyone agrees on what needs to happen, make it easier for teams to deliver. Identify everything that slows them down and determine what you can remove quickly. Historically, with good intentions, rules were implemented to improve quality and control spending. Often these evolved into bureaucracy that doubles and triples what it takes for IT to deliver. Attack the bureaucracy and reduce technical debt to free up delivery.

22

Clarify who gets to decide what.

Decision-making is a great place to start simplifying. Peter Weill, professor at the MIT Sloan school of management, taught me to simplify governance by clarifying who gets to decide what. When teams understand boundaries, they don't waste time reinventing, they know where they are empowered to innovate and where they should build contributions from other teams. Good boundaries help people feel safe, avoid waste, and move faster.

23

Help teams adopt everything already decided.

Don't waste time trying to decide what is already done. For example, define a modern engineering process, but don't have each team decide their own. There is a whole chapter coming up on modern practices. To truly empower teams to go faster, make sure they understand how and why common practices help them. Make them easy to adopt. Don't just teach the new practices. Like defining the vision, explain why they need to work differently and how it will simplify and improve their experience.

24

Remove layers between IT and business.

Many IT organizations structure account management-type layers between business decision-makers and IT delivery teams. These layers are meant to help translate requirements, but at the speed we need to work, especially to adopt Agile practices, this structure will slow you down. Reallocate these people to more delivery capacity, and engage business subject matter experts directly with teams prioritizing and grooming items in your development team backlog.

25

Remove management layers to improve clarity.

Like in the previous lesson, more layers in management can slow teams down and muddle communication clarity. Again, reallocating middle management to more delivery capacity helps you improve speed and clarity, without increasing costs. The appropriate manager to employee ratios vary by role, but fewer layers is critical. Side benefit: middle management is usually the most resistant to adopting culture change.

26

Empower teams to change their plans.

Don't require teams to get permission to make appropriate changes. Unless it impacts a dependency with another team, allow everyone to update and recommunicate plans as they learn. Include business subject matter experts in the decisions. Regularly help teams resolve dependency conflicts, making sure everyone understands proposed changes, and focusing on what is best for the company and customers.

27

Evolve to future organizational roles thoughtfully.

Modern teams need a different balance of roles compared to historic IT teams. Over time we reduced the number of analysts, generic PMs, infrastructure specialists, testers and relationship managers, while adding people with skills in development, data science and security. And our network expertise changed to focus on internet edge and wireless networks. To reduce anxiety, explain the future balance early. Help employees develop new skills. Outsource the roles that will reduce, as people move or there is attrition.

28

Govern ALL IT investment including shadow.

Embrace the innovation happening outside of IT. Don't call it shadow IT. Consider it all part of your team. Identify duplication. Help with dependencies. Share. Don't try to move it to IT. Show your CEO and CFO the value of them engaging in, or delegating to you, the prioritization across ALL IT investments. Use Technology Business Management (TBM) to understand where all the investments are. Using a product like Apptio greatly simplifies this process.

29

Ensure activity isn't confused with progress.

Measure progress toward the vision, not the activities required to get there. Don't celebrate a release. Celebrate the impact of the release as it achieves the desired impact. Don't focus on how many experiments failed. Celebrate the learnings from them that are accelerating progress. Don't reward people for working long hours or completing tasks. To better incent behavior, recognize and reward outcomes and learnings that accelerate progress. Do not reward activity alone.

30

Avoid the attraction of shiny objects.

It is natural for techies to be fascinated by new technology. The latest tech can be useful in solving real problems. But not always. Help teams focus. Technology shouldn't be applied for technology's sake. As author and Harvard professor Clayton Christensen would say, make sure you are providing a job a customer wants done. Likewise, people may attach importance to highly visible activities within your company. Help teams understand real versus perceived importance by connecting how progress helps the vision.

Chapter Four

Debunk the Myths Holding You Back

In early 2013, I was just returning to my office at the Microsoft Redmond campus, when my phone rang. It was Kevin Turner's administrative assistant. At the time, about half the employees at Microsoft reported up to Kevin, and it was not normal to get time with him.

I heard, "Jim, can you come to Kevin's office right now?"

I answered, "Of course," like I had any other choice, but then I added, "Can you tell me why?"

A pause inspired a thrill of panic in me.

"He will tell you when you get here."

I won't try to explain all that went through my mind on the way over to Kevin's office.

I soon discovered that our CIO, Tony Scott, had decided to leave the company to take care of a family situation. Kevin told me that he wanted me to play the interim CIO while they conducted a search for the best person for the job.

Suddenly, my peers worked for me. Kind of. Temporarily. Scarily. Fortunately, I didn't want the job. My next career goal was to go back into the product groups. So, I pulled my peers together and asked their permission to play the role. I said we couldn't afford to lose the momentum we'd started. The company couldn't afford for us to pause while they found us a new leader. We determined to accelerate our progress, so we could better set up our new leader when that someone was found. We drove a new mantra, "Create tomorrow, deliver today," recognizing it had to be both simultaneously. I got to evangelize a new narrative to the organization, starting with many beliefs that had to change.

Seven months later, after exhausting other options and seeing all of our material progress, I was asked to take on the official CIO title without the word "interim." By then I was too invested to say no, and could now start making bigger changes, giving the team permission to break some more old norms.

31

Myth: accelerate what we've always done.

Just doing the same things faster will never gain the momentum you need. For culture and pace to change, directly address the problems with how work has always been done. Understand the practices people hold onto as sacred, so you can proactively debunk them. This isn't easy. People will fight material change. Get key influencers to adopt modern ways of working. Engage the willing. Recognize and reward that behavior so others want to follow.

32

Myth: Going fast will sacrifice uptime.

Fast and uptime aren't necessarily mutually exclusive. Fast can add risk so you need to manage the risks better, and ensure you can always recover quickly. Automate provisioning and release to eliminate manual errors while improving speed. Measure real uptime, not IT service availability. Is the business capability completing successfully? Other than during the transition, I don't recommend bimodal IT (where some go fast while others focus on uptime). Focus everyone on speed AND uptime.

33

Myth: internal businesses are IT's customers.

There are no customers or suppliers inside a company. Real customers buy or use your company's products. Trying to create the role of customer internally just creates confusion around the setting of appropriate metrics. Instead, IT must work collaboratively with the rest of the company to deliver for real customers. IT needs to feel as much ownership for the business outcomes as their business partners, measuring success with the same business metrics.

Myth: the cloud makes IT unnecessary.

Why make changes if IT is just going away? The only people who believe this myth don't understand the scope of IT and all the new demands on IT today. Sure, many things go away with cloud services. That is good as it allows IT a chance to meet all the new demands and opportunities. Democratize BI and focus instead on curating data for users. Adopt SaaS, avoiding customizations. Target where you really must be unique. Move to the cloud and retire data centers. Leverage AI to improve productivity.

35

Myth: ITIL isn't necessary with Agile.

As you accelerate, don't ignore the good principles in historic practices. Do challenge and eliminate bureaucracy, but don't eliminate ITIL processes completely. You still need change management, incident management, problem management, etc., but simplify and streamline the processes so they add value for fast teams. For example, automation and new cloud capabilities will simplify capacity management while helping to reduce overall risk.

36

Myth: multitasking helps you go faster.

We've learned personally that we can't be our best when multitasking, such as driving and texting. Likewise, when teams attack too many priorities at once, productivity drops and errors increase. Go faster with less risk of error by focusing on the vital few. Pick the most important efforts to do first, taking on new items as they finish. Always make progress. A well-managed backlog keeps you from ever stalling.

37

Myth: don't fix what isn't broken.

Change your definition of broken. Even if something is working well, if it is slowing you down, assume it is broken. You may even need to break some things to make progress, to build momentum or just to get appropriate attention. This is especially true for rules that are entrenched in your old culture. Agitate for the right change. Fix everything that slows you down.

Myth: control is necessary for security.

This is a common belief, especially around physical controls. Our new reality recognizes that these controls still need to exist, but they don't need to be your data centers or only controlled by your people. Ensure controls are still in place, and simplify your security management by outsourcing appropriate controls to cloud providers who have more sensors and controls than you can do yourself. Extend your monitoring, but give up some control to get more control.

39

Myth: public cloud is less secure.

This was once true. Today it is easy to show that public clouds are at least as secure as what any company can do efficiently alone. Consider the significant additional sensors and the benefits from analyzing security events across millions of customers using huge investments in data science to improve security. No company can keep up alone. Build a shared responsibility model with cloud providers around security. You are still accountable, and own some tasks, but share many tasks with capable cloud providers.

Myth: public cloud is more expensive.

There are many who still believe this. When I dig in, I always find they are not looking at total cost. Include all costs, not just what is in your budget. Stop analyzing incremental costs such as virtual machine (VM) rates. Instead, change to a cloud perspective. Save more by eliminating the need for VMs rather than reducing their rate. Leverage cloud capabilities to materially reduce total costs while dramatically accelerating delivery.

Chapter Five

Move to the Public Cloud Faster

When Satya took over running Microsoft's cloud business a couple of years before he was promoted to CEO, he implemented some significant changes as he discusses in his book, *Hit Refresh.* One thing he wanted was better direct customer feedback. As a proxy, he asked me to attend his weekly product review meetings and play the role of enterprise customer. This meant expanding my connections with my IT peers at our customers around the world, and driving our own internal deployments faster so we could provide the feedback he wanted. As a very early adopter of the public cloud, we made a lot of mistakes. There were few other companies to learn from deeply. We started to go before Microsoft's cloud was ready. In hindsight, that push helped make it ready.

We made a lot of assumptions in the beginning, and only some of them held true over time. By pushing the edge, we made progress but also stubbed our toes and learned a ton. In the summer of 2016, when we were 60 percent migrated, I remember asking Rick Stover, who led our shared infrastructure services team, "We have a schedule to migrate faster this year, but didn't we already do the easy stuff? Isn't the rest going to be more difficult?" He reminded me that everything didn't work back when we started. He said, "We do have the hard stuff left, but we'll go faster now that we know what we're doing." And he was right. The migration accelerated, getting to over 90 percent in less than a year, and beating our aggressive schedule and cost savings plans.

A good example of our learning was around pre-production environments. When the team told me that we were closing an old data center housing only test environments. I thought I was brilliant by insisting we move it all to Azure instead of keeping it on premise in space they'd allocated in one of our new data centers. We moved it fast, closed the data center and saved a lot of money. Then we discovered that we'd moved things that didn't need to be moved. We turned off what wasn't being used to cut the waste. Then we saved even more by recognizing that test environments weren't used around the clock. We leveraged the snooze feature in Azure to automate whole environments so we could turn them off in the evening, and turn them back on the next morning. We cut our costs by a third. This was only the start until we learned more.

In trying to get the incentives right, I moved accountability for the Azure spend to the teams that owned the services rather than keeping the accountability with the central infrastructure team who could only influence some of the costs. I didn't move the budget or cross charge, but kept track of costs as part of our migration dashboard. Teams had to reduce in other areas if they overspent their cloud forecast, while getting to reallocate any savings if they could drive more efficiency in their cloud usage. This opened the flood gates for more innovation.

Soon teams were using test automation to provision the capacity as part of a test pass, executing the test, and then turning everything back off. This allowed no persistent test environments. They also focused on their production usage. Previously provisioned capacity for failover or peak capacity were turned off with automation to turn it on when needed, driving further savings. If an environment was needed to validate a fix, a team could take a snapshot of the production environment, deploy the fix, test it, and then even point production at this new environment and turn off the previous production capacity. The agility for teams with the cloud was amazing. And the net effect of costs? After effectively migrating everything, our Azure bill was less than our savings from pre-migration spend on just data center hosting and what we saved on infrastructure operations. The hardware costs we spent so much time comparing in the beginning, were now effectively zero.

We documented what we did, and what the team continues to learn. Detail lesson writeups can be found at Microsoft.com/itshowcase.

41

Identify appropriate workloads to move first.

Don't spend too much time analyzing before you start. Leverage a good catalog of apps and services. Start by moving simple apps or services: low regulatory impact, less mission critical, fewer interfaces, less latency sensitive. Also consider those that need new hardware or have larger non-production environments. These return the largest savings and have less friction to move. Get started and learn.

42

Go. Cloud migration can fund itself.

Don't wait for permission. Start full cloud migration now. Move packaged apps to SaaS, removing unnecessary customizations. Convert apps and capabilities to PaaS wherever possible. Containerize legacy and move to IaaS where it isn't practical to convert yet. Move first the workloads with clear savings. Learn and use the migration savings to move more. Where possible use the savings to fund both migrations and refactoring the portfolio to take advantage of the cloud.

43

Move budget accountability to application teams.

Maybe the best decision I made to improve migration was moving the accountability for Azure spend to the teams that could more impact the spend. It changed the incentives. Deep reporting on cloud utilization allowed teams to optimize their cloud spend. The incentive to drive the optimization increased when savings allowed them to accelerate other progress for their business partners. This incentive drove amazing innovation, leading to many other lessons.

Cloud migration isn't about cost savings.

The real value of public cloud migration is in agility and new capabilities possible with cloud scale, not cost savings. We did have savings and used them to accelerate the migration, based on a budget assuming a fast migration. But learnings and innovations through the migration drove dramatic improvements in our agility, and value that we could not have delivered before the cloud. Adjustable capacity removed friction. With effectively all our on-premise environment migrated, significant new opportunities arose.

45

Measure migration progress through on-premise reduction.

As we migrated, we learned that counting in the cloud is different than on-premise. After migrating almost 55k on-premise VMs, we used less than 20k Azure VMs. The difference went to SaaS apps, PaaS services, or just weren't needed anymore with our new agility. The best way to measure migration is measuring from where we started on-premise to what's left. This means at 95% migrated, only 5% of our original capacity on-premise was left.

Eliminate static test environments through automation.

Where pre-production environments are still needed, we learned not to leave them on outside working hours. The Azure snooze feature could automate shutdown and restart as necessary. Then we learned to just automate provisioning the test environments as part of a test run, deleting all after the test, so no permanent preproduction environments are needed. This became the standard. Less cost and more agility.

47

Rethink your definition of an application.

Savings can quickly fund new investments needed to refactor some apps with cloud services. For example, an app that employees used to update their personal information was replaced by a process initiated by end-users that starts a cloud service, allows input, writes updates through Azure Integration Services directly to our HR module in SAP, and then turns everything off. No persistent app. Also, new microservices and consistent APIs helped simplification.

Infrastructure teams need new cloud goals.

After migration, significant infrastructure work goes away or is self-service enabled for app teams. Give opportunities to infrastructure people for new security and app roles. Those that are left can upgrade wireless networks for a better modern workplace, make these networks internet-only, or govern cloud usage for application teams, advising them where to improve, and leveraging templates to simplify adoption while ensuring security controls.

49

Empowerment drives greater application team responsibility.

Application teams need new skills to best handle their new empowerment. Historically, infrastructure teams provisioned new capacity, built databases, and managed storage and backups for the application teams. To effectively go fast in the cloud, application teams automate these capabilities themselves seamlessly using templates from infrastructure advisory teams to automate the provisioning, resiliency, security, and other capabilities for their cloud applications and services.

50

After migration continue to eliminate IaaS.

Ideally, you don't need to lift and shift anything from compute and storage on-premise to the equivalent commodity compute and storage in the cloud. The reality is you will containerize and move some legacy applications because they are integrated to something else you want to move. Come back and optimize these to get more value later with new PaaS capabilities, and simple microservices.

Chapter Six

Modernize Legacy Practices to Simplify Acceleration

In 2011, two years before I was asked to be Microsoft's CIO, I got an offer from Amazon for what was the equivalent of their CIO role. Fortunately, Amazon recruiting took forever to get the actual offer to me, so delayed that Bryan Valentine, the Jeff Bezos direct report I would work for, felt so bad he drove the offer letter to my house personally.

Meanwhile, I'd told Tony Scott, Microsoft's then CIO that I was getting an offer from Amazon. Tony and Kevin arranged for me to meet Steve Ballmer to get his perspective on the opportunity. I'd been in a lot of meetings with Steve over the years, but never a 1:1 about me.

I was scheduled for a twenty-minute meeting in Steve's office on a Saturday morning. I told Steve right away my reasoning in even looking at an offer from Amazon. Beyond my family's passion for traveling the world, we had no desire to ever leave our Seattle home, and I loved being in IT in the software industry where our role included product feedback and customer engagement. If I was ever going to leave Microsoft, my choices were limited. Amazon was on a very short list at the time. I also explained that for all the reasons I loved Microsoft, we could learn some lessons from Amazon. They had better customer focus, they integrated and treated IT as part of their product teams, and had modernized many legacy practices. Steve was curious about my perspective. We debated some myths and talked about how legacy simplification could accelerate our progress. Ninety minutes later, he realized he was going to be late for a commitment with his wife, but he had more questions. He asked me to walk with him to his car. And then continuing to ask questions, had me get in his big white SUV so he could drive me around to my car. He committed to champion the issues I raised if I would stay and help drive them.

I decided to stay. I was skeptical whether Steve would follow through, but determined I was going to make a difference for the better anyway. A couple weeks later, I got a call from J Ritchie who led Microsoft's employee compensation process. J told me that he was driving a project for Steve to improve employee compensation. He wasn't sure why, but Steve had told him that he needed to take my input on the plan. I realized if Steve was doing this, I had all the support I needed to drive hard for modernization. Microsoft misses Steve's unbridled enthusiasm, but Satya continues to push for a lot of the changes I was hoping to see in the culture at Microsoft: looking at everything from a customer's perspective, focusing on inclusion of all perspectives, working together as one company, and providing people opportunities to make a positive impact on the world.

I knew that IT had an opportunity to help the company make radical improvements for the good, but we needed to change ourselves quickly to do that. We looked at modern practices, not just for developing, integrating and implementing software, but how we incorporated design thinking to enhance what we were doing, and simplifying adoption for our users by deploying smaller bite-size changes more often rather than huge releases that required massive change management. Satya also helped me realize that we needed to stop feeling good about our brilliant engineering to get Microsoft and other third-party products to work for us, and instead drive better accountability with the appropriate product teams. If we needed to add glue code to make it work, then many of our customers would need to add the same, which was bad.

We had a lot to transform. Modernizing how we worked not only helped us go faster with better results, but eliminating layers and fixing bad processes reduced our costs and increased the level of trust we received from the rest of the company.

First consolidate or eliminate everything possible.

With each data center closure, we found material capacity we could just turn off. We learned to monitor usage more proactively to simplify first. Don't just consolidate data centers to the cloud. Also, streamline teams doing similar work, and eliminate duplicate application instances and infrastructure processes. Containerize or convert legacy apps and services. Expect at least 20 to 30 percent-plus just from simplification.

52

Recognize Agile requires a mindset transformation.

There are many books that teach Agile practices. I'll just focus on our lessons learned. First, Agile is a culture change itself. Real Agile adapts to changing priorities and learns as you go. Build a minimum viable product, and then iterate. Ideas from any learnings can get prioritized immediately into the backlog you are grooming. Cultivate a mindset to experiment. Fail fast, learn and use data from telemetry to make decisions.

53

Implement real Agile, not shorter waterfalls.

Transformation is not going faster with the same historical IT practices, or getting more done by just working longer hours, or adding capacity with more lower cost resources. Don't just overlay what teams knew historically on top of Agile practices. Using shorter waterfalls completely misses the point. Fundamental change is required. Dedicated coaches can help teams really transform faster.

54

Telemetry provides data to make decisions.

Possibly the most important thing I learned in our transformation was the importance of telemetry. Implemented everywhere, you see immediately when something isn't working, so you can fail fast. You can see how customers and all users are interacting with your system to quickly iterate improvements. You see the results of your experiments. I don't know how we'd have thrived without telemetry. You can do this while protecting privacy by collecting data about behaviors, not necessarily who did what.

Cultivate a DevOps mindset, not roles.

DevOps isn't a separate role or separate team. It is the way everyone needs to think and act going forward. With a DevOps mindset, everyone plans how something will run, while building it, not later. They drive for automation, security, and integration. They design telemetry to ensure it runs well. They understand live site reviews and maniacally drive to root cause.

Agile everywhere, not just software development.

Agile practices can apply to all teams, not just software development. To simplify everywhere, we combined Agile practices with streamlined meeting conduct to infrastructure teams, security teams, live site reviews, business stakeholder backlog reviews--everywhere. Patrick Lencioni's book, *Death by Meetings*, is great for overhauling meetings, including keeping meetings engaging, and separating tactical from strategic topics.

57

Consider where standardizing across teams accelerates.

Look for standardization that optimizes across teams, while still allowing for empowerment. For example, you can simplify estimating by making sprint team sizes consistent. And enable dependent releases by implementing consistent release schedules across teams. We planned dependent integrations to line up quarterly while allowing individual sprints to last two or three weeks. Also standardizing development tools allows loaning of sprint teams to the highest priority business needs.

58

Rotate roles for balance and cleanup.

We adopted a practice to not fully schedule two people per sprint per team. These two are on call for any production issues owned by that team, shielding the rest of the team to complete sprint priorities uninterrupted. When there are no issues, they knock off technical debt backlog items. This also helps people plan their personal lives for when they might be on call for a production issue.

59

Complex integrations slow down your progress.

Simplify releases by using switches to turn on or off new capabilities. Often, this allowed us to decouple dependent releases. One team can release with their capability turned off, then turn it on when the rest releases. This also reduces release risk since capabilities can be turned off quickly if telemetry ever shows issues. Switches are later removed or consolidated to streamline code. Switches can provide for smaller more regular changes to simplify user adoption as well.

60

Decision-making: discuss, debate, decide, do.

Simplifying your decision-making also supports going faster. Help teams understand where you are in the decision process. Don't waste time debating options or trying to decide until the problem and options are clear. Problems well-defined are half-solved. Once decided, everyone should agree, or disagree and commit, and then move on. Don't let debate continue after decisions, unless material new information is found. (Credit to Dave Gasiewicz for the alliteration of "Ds".)

Chapter Seven

Transformation is Measured by Business Success

About the time Satya was promoted to CEO and I became CIO officially, one product group leader came up with a plan to dramatically improve customer support for his online service. He approached me, asking that I move all our customer support systems (for all products) to him so he could iterate more quickly. I liked his goal, but had commitments to other product teams so couldn't just move everything to him. I committed resources to work with his team to accomplish what he needed. He escalated to Satya, asking him to tell me to move everything.

Satya's response changed how I thought about my role. He and I agreed that IT needed to respond at the pace he needed for his transformation. Satya recognized that there was a lot of IT-like work happening across different teams throughout the company, outside the single IT organization that I now ran. He told me my job as CIO was to govern it all, whether it was in my team or not. He told me my accountability was to rationalize all "IT" investments, optimizing at the Microsoft level and "outsourcing" development to product teams if it would accelerate his transformation, without giving up accountability for ensuring we drove to the right outcomes.

Taking the new charter, we quickly mapped efforts across the company by business process, identifying similar or duplicate investments. A chart was born with business capabilities as the rows, and organizations across Microsoft as columns. We mapped north star visions to the rows, and started consolidating teams by row between columns to accelerate work. We knew the chart had limited fidelity in some areas outside my team, but it was directionally right so we didn't slow down. As I evangelized the ambition, I drew out the chart on whiteboards for audiences across the company, always drawing a smaller green box around my team and a blue box around the whole chart, telling everyone that I now feel accountable for the blue box.

Our lack of branding skills in IT showed as the name "Blue Box" stuck, symbolizing what we were working to make real. And I did end up moving part of the customer support systems to a product team, though a different one from the original request. We saw an opportunity to combine it with work from windows telemetry to create what is now an Artificial Intelligence (AI) based chat bot available online to help customers around the world. The bot learns from data, including how human customer support people are answering questions, and how customers are responding. It is taking over more and more of the call and chat volume, though customers can always ask for a human.

The moral of the Blue Box story was that the transformation was measured by real business outcomes in each row of the chart, rather than focusing on the columns of who did what, or how it was done. Leveraging data to help customers get their questions answered, and answered correctly and quickly, or more importantly, eliminating the need to ask in the first place, was just one example of the business value we were driving. Think about what can make a huge impact to help your customers, to help your employees, to transform your products to disrupt your industry, in addition to optimizing your operations. All of this should add to your vision of what you are trying to accomplish.

There are a few lessons I learned in how we got the rest of the company to change thinking that allowed us to make progress toward the vision. In the model above, the finance organization was a great ally in looking at all investments across the company and eliminating duplication. Finance is always looking for ways to optimize investments, and they were critical in achieving the empowerment to drive change outside of my direct reporting IT organization.

Another model was using data to motivate change by recognizing organizations that were quick to adopt. While publishing dashboards to highlight groups across the company that were doing well, we also showed the whole list, not just those doing the best, motivating those on the bottom to improve. For example, when we were trying to make data available for cross-company business intelligence (BI), we ran into some who didn't want to share the data they had. There may have been a fear of giving up power by sharing their data, but when we started publishing who was sharing and who wasn't yet, everyone quickly was motivated to participate, especially after Satya congratulated those who were first to participate.

61

Agility is wasted without appropriate results.

A great culture that supports change, and teams that can work with speed and agility, are worthless if they are not delivering transformative, tangible results. I'm sharing lessons I've learned to modernize IT in this book, but it is all a waste without real business success. In this chapter I attempt to define and give examples of success . . . or not success.

62

Historical IT metrics aren't success measures.

Historically, IT measured success using compliance, uptime, and delivery: on time, on scope, on budget. These are still worth tracking, but should not define success. It's the wrong incentive for IT to deliver just what is asked of them. Instead, define success based on bona fide business improvement, not IT delivery. And measure end-to-end processes working as expected, not uptime of IT services.

63

Engage business to define true success.

Measuring business improvement is complicated. Some business partners will really understand their power metrics as part of overall company success. Others will optimize for individual team success, even at the expense of the whole company. Push for metrics that define true success, for the company and your customers. This allows everyone to innovate to drive real improvements at the right level.

Make sure you drive real transformation.

Digital transformation is not going paperless, or building new mobile applications. It is rethinking what you do completely, dropping efforts that are no longer worthy, and prioritizing new and existing growth opportunities that can help you disrupt. It requires new levels of agility and innovation from everyone, and to get there faster, it requires simplifying legacy environments and API enabling everything for agility.

65

Expand vision to each company process.

Build north star visions for each part of your company to connect to the overall vision. This provides focus, and a way for everyone to attach to the overall vision. These "parts" can be cut by major business processes, product lines or experiences, but do not just follow organizational boundaries. Think of all the apps or capabilities for each part as a product that you are improving iteratively. Plan based on the products, not projects. Align visions for these products ignoring org lines, allowing you to understand and eliminate duplication.

66

Find new value in existing data.

Can you combine data you already have to create new value? Is there a business model hidden in what you discard? For example, we had years of enterprise sales opportunity data. We were about to purge it since all the opportunities were long past. Then we discovered the data was useful to train a machine-learning model that accurately predicted success of any new sales opportunities. This opened up many new ideas.

67

Predict success and then improve it.

Big data can make the future more predictable and less uncertain. Spending time on real value here is a reason we go faster elsewhere. Once we determined how to reasonably predict success of sales opportunities, we attacked related, but more complicated, AI problems. What actions can we recommend to improve the forecasted success? Can we completely automate the whole sales forecasting process to free up sellers to have more direct time with customers?

Find insights connecting data across processes.

Marketing pioneered A/B testing, using experiments to determine value. Any analysis of user behavior can create new insight, especially when connecting across processes. Using AI to look at behaviors and actions, we improved our marketing model by connecting marketing-qualified leads all the way through sales to orders. Connecting the end results of a lead all the way through allowed us to improve our model for rating marketing leads, increasing their value.

69

Clean up your data for decision-making.

In driving transformation, ensure you have mechanisms to keep your data clean, improving its usefulness in decision-making. Incent people to share data. This removes redundancy and speeds learning, especially data that hurts by identifying previous truths that are actually false. Transformed processes should identify data issues quickly and prioritize them in the sprint backlogs. And, clarifying data ownership accountabilities will help drive consistency.

70

Optimize the appropriate manual operations tasks.

In a digital transformation, prioritize what you automate based on what adds the most value, rather than just digitizing all manual tasks. If optimizing one process doesn't improve the end-to-end process, it should become a relatively low priority unless it is keeping you from scaling your business. Eliminating steps altogether is better than automating them, but improving the end-to-end process is better than eliminating or just automating the steps.

Chapter Eight

Accelerate Without Sacrificing Security and Compliance

In 2000, the Wall Street Journal reported that Microsoft had been hacked. While Microsoft disagreed with the facts of the article, seeing the impact of what could have happened was a wake-up call. Security jumped in priority immediately and stayed there because we started finding more vulnerabilities and needed to change how we thought about security. This priority highlighted new practices, skills and tools to improve security in our products, and our ability to protect ourselves and our customers. Some product teams skipped whole release cycles, dedicating capacity to addressing better security.

But by 2006, I was frustrated by our slower overall pace, feeling we were not getting the balance right. Security was getting in the way of delivery. When our Chief Information Security Officer left the company, I was asked to take the position. In hindsight, I know I was not qualified. I did not get the job because I was a security expert. I believe I was given the job because I complained the most about security keeping us from going faster. I could hear the unspoken congratulations, "OK Jim, you fix it."

I embraced the new team, curious about how I could make a difference. My eyes were opened. I had no idea how easy it was to compromise a company's defenses, even if they were careful. My new team was looking to me to sponsor what they needed from the rest of the company. I understood how important it was for the future of Microsoft to get this right. I also remembered how frustrated I'd been with security before my eyes were opened. I determined that I needed a mission where appropriate security and great productive experiences could co-exist, where it would be an AND, not an OR. It took a long time to articulate this well to all stakeholders and make progress. The best choice I eventually made was to hire a real security leader, Bret Arsenault, for the team as I took on more responsibilities in addition to the security organization. Bret hired and developed one of the best security teams in the world, even if they do all keep tape over their laptop cameras.

I was constantly amazed by the team as the world evolved. Microsoft was on the list of most attacked entities on the planet. We played chess with very real adversaries trying to disrupt us, or steal secrets, always needing to keep a few moves ahead. We collected and ingested over 20 billion events a day into our AI based engine to look for anomalies.

Modern practices and the cloud were game changers for us to stay ahead. Bret's team helped design AI based products like Windows Defender ATP for huge steps forward. Like the cloud migration, we learned a lot on the journey, including where we needed to help all our teams better understand security, and build it in from the start. Sophisticated red team/blue team exercises helped us identify new threat vectors, but we continued to prioritize basic hygiene first, and then prepare for more advance persistent threats (ATPs).

Sometimes the ATP preparation was surreal, like when Satya asked us to release Sony's movie *The Interview* on Xbox Live on Christmas day in support of free speech. We prepared to counter a possible attack in response. We knew from forensics of the Sony hack what we might expect. Authorities identified ranges where we should look for an attack to come from. We collaborated on strategy with Google's security team as they prepared to launch at the same time on YouTube. All of it felt like I was in a movie myself, and all of it was important example to take security very seriously.

Everyone is accountable for faster security.

With the sophistication of bad adversaries today, everyone must understand and feel accountable for security. Otherwise one incident can derail all your other efforts. Security teams should help everyone learn to stay secure, not try to do it alone. All teams should work with security teams as advisors. Security is not the enemy of fast when we work together. Only together can we succeed.

72

Fast and secure can be complementary.

Design security in from the start, so it improves speed. Help teams understand how to be secure, so security never slows them down. Empowering teams to use security tools themselves limits the risk of finding security issues too late in a release. Tools such as code review tools can be automated into every test pass during sprint team iterations. Leverage templates and scripts to ensure security controls are active and operating as expected.

Prioritize security hygiene to minimize risk.

Ninety percent of security incidents are prevented with focus on good security hygiene. Almost every hack you've read about in the news was not some sophisticated attack, but rather was enabled by someone not taking security hygiene seriously. Stay current. Stay patched. Manage strong identities. Encrypt your data. Establish good monitoring, incident management and recovery processes. Leverage templates and scripts to ensure there is no configuration drift.

74

Secure important data wherever it goes.

Network boundaries no longer provide the same protection. Critical data goes everywhere on mobile devices and through APIs with partners. Assume your network is compromised. Prioritize protecting data instead. Classify the data. Make sure your controls are designed to protect the data wherever it goes. Isolate as appropriate. Detect when anything is trying to compromise your protections. Practice how you respond and recover quickly.

75

Identity is the new security boundary.

Network used to be the boundary and I would still consider software-defined networks, but the future focus is strong identity. Include user, device, app and data identities. Implement multi-factor authentication, and plan to eliminate the use of passwords completely. There should be no persistent elevated access for any user. Instead have a simple process to grant temporary access to approved people when they need it. Ensure devices are healthy to enforce strong user identities. Apps and data should understand access restrictions.

76

Log everything. Capture all relevant information.

Security is unique in that you may consider duplication of roughly equivalent security products because they each give you overlapping but not complete views of what is happening in your environments. Log and consolidate every action by users, devices and applications, every access attempt to data. Timely ingestion of huge amounts of data is solvable today to consolidate all these events. Plan for time to tune out all the false positives.

77

Use AI to stay moves ahead.

To extend the chess analogy I started earlier, always plan multiple moves ahead. When you see a move, anticipate where it could go next and what plan might be behind it. Look for anomalies in regular behavior. All of this is a great problem for AI to rationalize across billions of actions to alert you to where security experts need to spend their precious time in analysis and response.

Prioritize security and great user experience.

Don't view these as a tradeoff. Find ways to do both. When security gets in the way, some users will actively try to work around security. Make doing the right thing simple so everyone will more easily help keep you secure. Capabilities like single sign-on and elimination of passwords are examples of strong security measures that also provide a better experience.

Simplify technical debt with every release.

When simplification becomes a mantra, when it is encouraged as part of everything you do from design to release, the complete portfolio of services run by IT gets less complicated over time, even while you are adding more and more capabilities. Simplification allows you to go faster AND drive more appropriate security.

80

Eliminate duplication to simplify compliance controls.

Another great place for simplification is control testing. GDPR, SOX, PCI, ISO, and other standards each have a set of controls to be tested. A lot of the controls overlap and you can simplify to test each control once, applying the test to all standards. Further, you should consider redesigning your controls to overlap more, allowing better consolidation and simplification.

Chapter Nine

Optimism and Persistence are Force Multipliers

I learned optimism from my mom. She's probably the most positive, outgoing person I've ever met. Everybody likes my mom, and our house was continually full of people stopping by to see her. She welcomed everyone and was always excited to see people, no matter what else was happening, how bad she felt, or how crummy her day had been. I watched how people responded to her, and wanted to take part in anything she did. I determined that I would at least try to emulate her positive view on life.

I learned persistence from my dad. Dad was the youngest of sixteen children from an immigrant lumberjack and his very busy wife. None of my dad's sisters and brothers went to college, and my dad wasn't on a path to do more before he met my mom. When I was born, he decided to go to college. I don't remember that most nights we ate rice with tomato sauce, but I do remember that dessert was a saltine cracker. I was four when my dad graduated. I saw that no matter what challenge was thrown at him, he didn't give up. He persevered working in construction to pay his way through college, working through issues to become a partner in a regional tax practice, and starting his own company when his partners decided to pursue a direction against his beliefs.

These lessons formed a foundation for who I am today. They taught me to persevere when I hit rough times, working to pay my own way through college, through the tough times and dead ends in my career, and to even not give up on my marriage after a counselor recommended that my wife and I divorce. I also saw my optimism rewarded when I learned along the way and didn't give up, such as recently celebrating our thirtieth wedding anniversary. The lessons also taught me to have fun with work as you go, and never wish your life away as some people can do just trying to get through demanding situations. Embrace the adversity, learn and find ways to enjoy the ride.

Make sure that your teams also have fun with you. A sense of humor is important. When appropriate, contrive events where you can include friends and families. Thank the families for their support of your employees.

If I could do my whole life over, the only thing I would change would be to apply some of these lessons earlier.

81

Accelerate by building optimism with persistence.

Healthy optimism doesn't ignore reality, but always uses a positive lens. People don't enjoy being around negativity. Meaningful purpose and clear vision drive out negativity. When you hit bumps, learn, then keep going to drive progress. Persistent progress builds optimism. Lead by starting with optimism and never showing discouragement. People are watching you, and how you react to challenges.

82

Identify the negativity holding you back.

A toxic environment is rules-focused, uses guilt to control, prioritizes the urgent but not important tasks, is not respectful of other teams you need to work with, and plays the victim role when anything bad happens. For the culture and speed you need to develop, do not tolerate these traits. Kill them wherever and whenever you see them. Have fun and make sure your team can balance and integrate their personal lives with their work.

83

Rescue yourself. Don't be a victim.

Ensure that you aren't the one holding back the team. If you can't be positive, at least don't be negative. Learn to trust people, knowing some will fail you. More will trust back. Confront failure and learn. If you feel like a victim, it isn't too late to change. Holding onto hurt only impacts you. Forgiveness frees you to move on without meaning everything is better. Forgive and move on.

84

Believe first. Deal with doubts later.

It is OK to believe in the future and still have doubts. Work them out as you go. Keep past negatives in the past. Learn from them, but always assume positive intent in others. When you see something that looks wrong, ask before going negative. Most of the time, you will find good intentions. A quick conversation can resolve misunderstandings.

Healthy conflict is a progress accelerator.

When everyone assumes positive intent, it is easier to have healthy conflict. No one is afraid to ask the hard questions. Small misunderstandings don't grow to mistrust. Small issues are resolved quickly and don't grow to become big issues. Eliminating this waste helps teams go faster, allowing everyone to focus on delivering what your company needs.

86

Eliminate ownership issues to avoid competition.

Ownership disputes are a common conflict that lowers productivity. When another team, either unknowingly or purposefully, does something that is your responsibility, you can fight about it, or you can choose to work together. Assume they have the right intentions. Figure out the best way forward together. The goal is to benefit your company and your customers, not who gets credit.

87

Learn from failure. Look for opportunities.

Winston Churchill said, "A pessimist sees difficulty in every opportunity. An optimist sees opportunity in every difficulty." What do you look for? Do you manage risk by looking for difficulties in opportunities? It is all about how you approach life. You are more likely to succeed if you look for ways to succeed, rather than trying to find reasons something will fail.

88

Perfection is the enemy of great.

If you wait for perfect, you won't just avoid great, you will fail because you were too slow. When is good, good enough? The answer is when there is something higher priority that you should do instead of improving on good. There are too many huge opportunities today to waste time perfecting everything. Reward progress, not perfection. Progress builds optimism.

Optimism and persistence improve executive presence.

People want to follow leaders who know they can succeed. People want to follow leaders who aren't going to give up. Executive presence is something that you know when you see, but can be hard to describe, let alone teach. A useful book to help improve executive presence is *All the Leader You Can Be* by Suzanne Bates.

Chapter Ten

It is All About
the People

People are the most important asset in any company. I needed to start this book talking about culture to set up any transformation, so I made this chapter on people the finale. Attracting, developing and retaining the best people and then molding them into a team is the most important part of what any leader does. I believe these lessons are some of the most important I had to learn.

For seven years before I started at Microsoft, at the company now called Accenture, I worked in different industries, learning not just how to implement big IT projects, but how different company cultures impact how we work. While at Microsoft, I ran multi-national teams, living in Tokyo and London for two years each. Trying to move quickly to consolidate processes, applications and data centers, I learned the hard way about the impact of many diverse cultures at work.

Once in Tokyo, I had a great idea how to streamline the local helpdesk. My direct reports were spread across Asia, but the leader of the Japan team, Tatsuya Arase (Tats), brought his helpdesk lead in to discuss the idea. This person didn't speak English, so Tats translated my idea. I should have noticed his facial expressions, but Tats told me he thought it was a clever idea. I was thrilled and asked how fast we could make it real. The next day a team-building event called a *shinbokai* was scheduled for the whole team of people based in Tokyo. Soon after I arrived, Tats brought the helpdesk leader up to me, drink in hand. He'd figured out a bit of English, and told me, "Your idea for helpdesk? Not so good for Japanese people." I was stunned, but Tats explained to me the importance of respect for hierarchy in their culture, but alcohol is an accepted excuse.

I now understood the purpose of *shinbokai*, and determined to always find people for my team who would tell me when I was doing something stupid. I learned to value the diverse perspectives and cultures on my team, and how to set expectations around using judgment to do what was right.

That was just one of the lessons about people. It made me curious about how to bring out the best in people. My wife taught me that psychologists define performance as a function of ability, motivation and environment. This book is intended to stretch your thinking about attracting and developing people with the abilities to work at the new pace, motivate them with a vision and a sense of purpose, and create the environment (culture) for them to be their best.

90

People are your most important asset.

These lessons started with culture on purpose, and need to end with the people involved. As a leader, you are only as successful as the people who surround you. Invest in them as individuals, and as a team. For building healthy teams, I highly recommend following Patrick Lencioni's practices in his book, *The Five Dysfunctions of a Team*.

91

Every hire should be an upgrade.

Never hire someone who doesn't have the potential to pass you. Consider this with every hiring decision. Look for attitude, passion, and drive as more important attributes than the specific expertise that can be learned. When interviewing, ask them to describe situations where they've had to handle conflict. Ask what they liked most about their best boss ever and about the best company culture they've ever experienced.

92

Find and develop learners not knowers.

Learning is better than knowing. As everything speeds up, the ability to learn is more and more important. The half-life of expertise is getting shorter, and the value of expertise is shrinking. To thrive, seek and grow people who can learn quickly and value learning over knowledge. Knowers slow you down by focusing more on who is right than on making progress.

93

Find and nurture judgment and courage.

There is no substitute for good judgment. To successfully move fast, leaders will need the ability to develop rational points of view and make decisions, often based on weak signals. If they always look to you for answers, you are the bottleneck. Find people who handle ambiguity well and can apply good judgment to these situations. Encourage healthy debate to develop these skills.

94

Find and reward people with grit.

Dr. Travis Bradberry, author and expert on emotional intelligence, defines grit as making mistakes, looking like an idiot, and trying again without flinching. It is trusting your gut, making calls you are afraid to make, keeping your emotions in check, giving more than you get, taking accountability for your actions, and being kind to people who are rude to you. Anyone can develop more grit with focus. Stronger teams will display grit.

95

Build diverse teams to improve results.

I learned this lesson the hard way, early in my career. Teams that all think like the leader are at risk. They may seem faster at first but fall short by missing out on ideas and perspectives to improve outcomes for your business. Seek out people who will tell you when you do something wrong. Listen to all perspectives to improve the team value. Leverage individual strengths to balance team weaknesses or gaps.

96

Interns and college hires bring energy.

Another form of diversity is hiring people who aren't stuck in legacy IT practices. College hires or professionals from outside of IT don't need to unlearn the way it has always been done. Their energy can also motivate the rest of the team if your culture supports it. A strong intern program helps you find the best college hires.

97

Don't treat every person the same.

Make sure you are fair and respectful. Recognize unconscious bias to improve. But know that people are different. Differences are good. And this also means that not everyone is motivated by what motivates you. Ask what people are passionate about, and what makes them feel appreciated. Leverage their passions to motivate them, and show appreciation in ways that are meaningful to them.

98

Repeat for clarity. People hear differently.

You think you are clear, but everyone else heard what you said through a lens based on their own experiences. Sometimes they hear what they want. Often, they hear what they expect, which may be different than your intent. Understand this reality. Repeat your message to build clarity. Use different channels to build clarity. Ask others to repeat the message to build clarity. Listen to validate.

99

Use judgment to avoid unintended consequences.

Leaders need to be clear on their intent. Anytime you design a process, or have a side discussion, consider what could go wrong. I remember someone stopping me in the hall to explain an idea. I told them it was interesting, only to find weeks later dozens of people working on the idea, "because Jim said to." If it doesn't seem right, it may not have been the leader's intent even if someone claims it is. Encourage all to use judgment to avoid people doing something just because.

100

Remember to re-recruit your best people.

While finding great new talent, don't forget to regularly re-recruit people you already have. In recruiting, part of the process is taking time to explain why they should want to come work with you. This isn't an activity only for recruits. Tell your people why they are valued, and make sure they understand why they should continue working with you.

Acknowledgements

I would be nothing without my faith and the people who molded me into the person I am today:

- First, my wife, Shannon, who gave up her career for a while to raise our three children and support me, before returning to get her doctorate in Psychology (and teach me a lot about myself as a test subject).

- My parents, Harvey and Sonia, who first introduced me to a deep, grace filled Christian faith as a foundation for everything.

- All three CEOs of Microsoft, Bill, Steve and Satya, who all challenged me to view IT within Microsoft from the lens of an enterprise customer, and drive feedback into our products.

- All the previous CIOs at Microsoft who taught me how to better measure and achieve success.

- My mentors, Craig Mundie and Qi Lu who helped me navigate Microsoft and think outside the box.

- Professors Dr. James Cash who invested in me long before I became a CIO, and Peter Weill who taught me that Digital Transformation is a CEO/Board topic rather than an IT topic, years before it was.

- Authors: Patrick Lencioni, Peter Drucker, Clay Christensen, John Wooden and Steven Covey who gave me ideas to get out of predicaments so often that I quote them without realizing it.

- The 13 different managers I had in my 24 years at Microsoft who all pushed me to do what I often felt was impossible.

- And finally, I want to thank all the people I got to work with over the years. The biggest reason I enjoyed my job so much was getting to work with such high quality people every day.

About the *Six-Word Lessons* Series

Legend has it that Ernest Hemingway was challenged to write a story using only six words. He responded with the story, "For sale: baby shoes, never worn." The story tickles the imagination. Why were the shoes never worn? The answers are left up to the reader's imagination.

This style of writing has a number of aliases: postcard fiction, flash fiction, and micro fiction. Lonnie Pacelli was introduced to this concept in 2009 by a friend, and started thinking about how this extreme brevity could apply to today's communication culture of text messages, tweets and Facebook posts. He wrote the first book, *Six-Word Lessons for Project Managers*, then started helping other authors write and publish their own books in the series.

The books all have six-word chapters with six-word lesson titles, each followed by a one-page description. They can be written by entrepreneurs who want to promote their businesses, or anyone with a message to share.

See the entire *Six-Word Lessons Series* at **6wordlessons.com**

89876828R00080